As Exceptional As Sapphires:

The Mother's Blessing and God's Favour Towards Women III

As Exceptional as Sapphires:
The Mother's Blessing & God's Favour Towards Women III

© Anne Hamilton, Donna Ho and Natalie Tensen 2021

Published by Armour Books
P. O. Box 492, Corinda QLD 4075 Australia

Interior Design and Typeset by Beckon Creative

ISBN: 978-1-925380-361

A catalogue record for this book is available from the National Library of Australia

Please note: the spelling, grammar and punctuation in this book are consistent with Australian language conventions.

All rights reserved. No part of this publication may be reproduced, stored in, or introduced into a retrieval system, or transmitted, in any form, or by any means (electronic, mechanical, photocopying, recording or otherwise) without the prior written permission of the publisher.

As Exceptional As Sapphires:

The Mother's Blessing and God's Favour Towards Women III

Anne Hamilton
Donna Ho

with prayers by
Dell Hamilton

and preface by
Natalie Tensen

Scripture quotations marked BSB are taken from the The Holy Bible, Berean Study Bible, BSB Copyright ©2016 by Bible Hub Used by Permission. All Rights Reserved Worldwide.

Scripture quotations marked ESV are taken from the ESV® Bible (The Holy Bible, English Standard Version®), copyright © 2001 by Crossway, a publishing ministry of Good News Publishers. Used by permission. All rights reserved

Scripture quotations marked KJV are taken from the King James Version of the Bible. Public domain.

Scripture quotations marked LSV are taken from Literal Standard Version of the Bible. Used by permission.

Scripture quotations marked NASB are taken from the New American Standard Bible®, Copyright © 1960, 1962, 1963, 1968, 1971, 1972, 1973, 1975, 1977, 1995 by The Lockman Foundation. Used by permission. (www.Lockman.org)

Scripture quotations marked NLT are taken from the Holy Bible, New Living Translation, copyright 1996, 2004. Used by permission of Tyndale House Publishers, Inc., Wheaton, Illinois 60189. All rights reserved.

Scripture quotations marked NIV are taken from the Holy Bible, New International Version®, NIV®. Copyright © 1973, 1978, 1984, 2011 by Biblica, Inc.™ Used by permission of Zondervan. All rights reserved worldwide. www.zondervan.com The "NIV" and "New International Version" are trademarks registered in the United States Patent and Trademark Office by Biblica, Inc.™.

Scripture quotations marked NKJV are taken from the New King James Version. Copyright © 1982 by Thomas Nelson, Inc. Used by permission. All rights reserved.

Scripture quotations marked PHPS are taken from the New Testament in Modern English © 1958, 1959, 1960 J.B. Phillips and 1947, 1952, 1955, 1957 The Macmillan Company, New York. Used by permission. All rights reserved.

Art and Photo Credits

Cover Image: Deposit Photos: olesiabilkei | Daddy puts on cute golden finger ring on daughter's little hand; snow by Brusheezy.com

p 3&10: superb photo | iStockphoto: natural loose sapphire gemstones

p 6–7: Pearl: | lightstock: Holding Hands in Prayer; New York Public Library | Unsplash: Full Disk Earth, Apollo 17, 1972

p 8: ozgurdonmaz: African Woman Praying; digitalskillet: Woman praying; camaralenta: Woman praying outdoors; THEPALMER: Woman Praying; ArtMari: Woman Praying; liliboas: crown of thorns | Getty Images

p 14: citalliance | dreamstime: beautiful mysterious girl; picryl: upper-beth-horon-village-joshua-165

p 37: artphotodima | canstockphoto: serious woman with Cleopatra makeup

p 51: Pearl | lightstock: the woman at the well

p 53: LUMO | lightstock: Jesus goes to a Quiet Place to Pray; The Sermon on the Mount; MariaDubova | iStockphoto: outdoor portrait

p 67: Kristy-Anne Glubish | Dollarphotoclub: women dancing

p 69: Photowitch | dreamstime: Bible scene with Mary of Bethany; jgroup | iStockphoto: He is Risen

p 81: Kevin Carden: butterflies coming from book

p 83: MillaFedotova | Dollarphotoclub: girl with sword

Floral & gem iconography by Beckon Creative www.beckoncreative.biz

Dedication

to
the grace-bringing 'five women'
who are building the Kingdom of Heaven

Also in this series

More Precious than Pearls:
The Mother's Blessing & God's Favour Towards Women

More Precious than Pearls with Study Guide
The Mother's Blessing & God's Favour Towards Women

As Resplendent as Rubies:
The Mother's Blessing &
God's Favour Towards Women II

As Resplendent as Rubies with Study Guide
The Mother's Blessing &
God's Favour Towards Women II

Jesus and the Healing of History

\# 1 Like Wildflowers, Suddenly

\# 2 Bent World, Bright Wings

\# 3 Silk Shadows, Rings of Gold

\# 4 Where His Feet Pass

\# 5 The Singing Silence

Contents

Preface	13
Introduction	15
1: Woman and Mother: City-Builder	16
Prayer for myself	32
Prayer for others	34
2: Woman and Mother: Nation-Shaper	36
Prayer for myself	47
Prayer for others	49
3: Woman and Mother: Paradigm-Shifters	52
Prayer for myself	64
Prayer for others	66
4: Woman and Mother: Chamberlain	68
Prayer for myself	79
Prayer for others	81
5: Woman and Mother: Torch-Bearer	84
Prayer for myself	95
Prayer for others	97
Endnotes	99

Preface

OUR WORLD HAS EMBARKED ON challenging times. As I write, numerous states around Australia are being shut down due to COVID-19, while Afghanistan is at war. According to news cycles our world is spiraling down, 24/7 news cycles of overwhelming fear. BUT this book is a segue in all that chaos. Like a beautiful rose in a garden of weeds or a gem shining through remnants of rubble. Find a tea and biscuit, sit in your favourite chair, and enjoy the faith and history woven so beautifully into these women's lives as stories we have not yet heard in our times are unearthed.

The narratives of women who have gone before us can continue to provide hope and encouragement in times of trouble. More than ever we need stories of women who overcame incredible odds and survived with soundness of mind, remaining persistent when loss, death and destruction came knocking. They reveal the narrow path of faith instead of the broad road of obeying orders for the sake of peace. These women did not let fear rule their choices. The world has known war, loss, and devastating times before—this book is a timely reminder in our comfortable, sometimes removed from reality, 21st century lives.

This however is also a time of opportunity. Like the saying, 'When life gives you lemons, make lemonade'—though, maybe slightly cynical—but still grit, determination and strength is forged in adversity. We shall all be tested in these times and what is exposed in humanity can be virtue or depravity—there is opportunity for both to prevail.

I desire virtue and truth, and the pages written by both Anne and Donna are beacons of hope, character, patience, resilience and kindness that they themselves have modelled—they truly are women of virtue in our world today, living heroes!

May this book go to bless countless people across our nation and world, with light, hope and the peace of heaven to overcome the chaos in our hearts and lives.

Peace be with you, my peace I give to you, do not give as the world gives,

BE NOT AFRAID.

Natalie

23 August 2021

Introduction

ONE MAJOR FOCUS OF THE first volume in this series, *More Precious than Pearls*, was the admiration in which the women of the Exodus are held by so many Jewish writers. Rightly so, for they were remarkable women of steadfast, tested faith: armour-bearers, watchmen, game-changers, gatekeepers and cupbearers.

The second volume, *As Resplendent as Rubies*, explores the role of women in the Bible who were kingmakers, visionaries, navigators, sentinels, mentors, culture-changers and even God-namers.

This third volume is about the women builders of Scripture and their overlooked role in advancing both earthly and heavenly kingdoms. It starts with the story of a woman who constructed three cities—the first cities built by a descendent of Abraham in the land promised to him by God. These cities turn out to be far from just any cluster of streets and houses—in later ages, it becomes clear the townplan was handed down as a blueprint straight from the sapphire floor of God's throne room. They are revealed as a civic prophecy of God's covenant with His people.

As you read these stories of Sheerah, Bithiah, Mahlah, No'ah, Hoglah, Milkah, Tirzah, Joanna and Deborah, may you be inspired to follow your own high calling as a Daughter of God. May you be blessed with blueprints for your own life that are *as exceptional as sapphires*.

1
Woman and Mother: City-Builder

1
Woman and Mother: City-Builder

Like grandfather, like granddaughter.

Sheerah only gets one line in Scripture. But don't let that fool you.

She was the granddaughter of Joseph of the coat of many colours. She was the daughter of his younger son, Ephraim. In one sense, she was also Jacob's granddaughter because, late in life, he adopted Ephraim.

For some unspecified reason, Ephraim returned to Canaan, the homeland of his father. The timing is unclear. Joseph had inherited a ridge at Shechem, gifted to him by Jacob. Perhaps Ephraim was sent to oversee this property. In addition it's possible that, because of the enormous power Joseph wielded as the steward of Pharaoh's household, he'd acquired assets in Canaan and so sent his son back home as an estate manager. Whatever the reason, Ephraim had settled in with his family.

Then two of his sons decided to try their hand at a spot of cattle-rustling. Now if you've seen any old westerns, y'all have probably guessed how the locals reacted to this raid. Yup, sure enough, they done got ornery with wild-west-style vengeance. Ephraim's boys were killed by the men of Gath—a town later to become famous for its resident giant, Goliath. Furthermore there's a heavy hint it didn't stop there and almost all the younger generation of Ephraim's family were wiped out.

It's a hard blow to lose children and grandchildren before their time. Ephraim was devastated.

> *Their father, Ephraim, mourned for them a long time, and his relatives came to comfort him. Afterward Ephraim slept with his wife, and she became pregnant and gave birth to a son. Ephraim named him Beriah because of the tragedy his family had suffered.*
>
> 1 Chronicles 7:22–23 NLT

The name, Beriah, means *tragedy, calamity*, or perhaps *weeping*. His sister, Sheerah, had a name that probably means *remnant*.[1] She appears on the scene and her life is summed up in a single comment:

> *Ephraim had a daughter named Sheerah. She built the towns of Lower and Upper Beth-horon and Uzzen-sheerah.*
>
> 1 Chronicles 7:24 NLT

That's all, on the surface, we know about her.

Yet she was responsible for a remarkable feat—constructing not just one, but three towns. She's the only woman in Scripture recorded as a city-builder. Remarkably, she wasn't a king with all of the resources of a national treasury behind her. Nor was she a priest, with a faithful following who'd like nothing better than to harness their talents in the creation of a beautiful sanctuary.

She may have had some advantage in being the granddaughter of Joseph and Asenath. Joseph, after all, had been the builder of storehouse-cities. Even if he was not a material help, she'd surely have been inspired by his prisoner-to-palace story. Perhaps the motivation behind her accomplishment was to carry on his legacy and to memorialise his role in preserving an entire nation during a seven-year famine.

Yet that does not diminish her achievement in raising up three cities in dangerous territory. She was a creator, a maker, a fabricator. We might even call her a 'city-smith'.[2] She was like Cain, the first city-builder, whose name means—among other things—*a maker* and *a smith*. In establishing more than one city, Sheerah was like Nimrod, the hunter famous for building four of them in Assyria.[3]

But Sheerah was also distinctively different from Cain and Nimrod—as different as the cities she built.

Are we meant to recall Cain, the first male city-builder, as we read this tiny fragment about the first female one? Are we meant to tally up the similarities and the differences? Both had lost brothers who'd been murdered. Of course, the circumstances were vastly different. Both Cain and Sheerah construct their cities in a land far away from their kin.[4] Both faced potential danger from those who might have wanted to kill them in revenge.

Although we have just a single bald sentence about Sheerah, we can tell a lot about her from the legacy she left.

First, let's note something unusual. Two of the three cities Sheerah built had the same name: Beth Horon. One was at the bottom of a hill, one at the top. They are three kilometers distant from each other and, until recently, they were connected only by a steep, narrow path with occasional steps cut into the bedrock. Sheerah essentially created a single city in two halves. Now that might not mean much to us today but, through this image of a divided civic 'body', Sheerah symbolised a covenant.[5]

Once again we find a faint and curious parallel with Cain. He named his city 'Enoch', *dedicated*, while Sheerah made a covenant *dedication* through her town plan. Cain's city might have been the very first in history. However Seerah's was not only the first in the Promised Land—an immense act of faith since it would be centuries before God's pledge to Abraham would come to fruition—but it was also the very last mentioned in the Hebrew Scriptures.

The closing book, time-wise, is Nehemiah. It's an historical account of the rebuilding of Jerusalem after the return of the exiles from Babylon. Beth Horon happens to be the very last location mentioned in that book. Right at the end of his story, Nehemiah throws in a final comment that he'd driven away the son of the high priest who was married to the daughter of Sanballat of Beth Horon.

Hidden in Scripture is the information that Sheerah's city has aspects of both first and last. It should remind us of Jesus, the Alpha and Omega. It's special. It would be special for the reason it was the first to be built in the Promised Land, even before the Hebrews came into possession of it, and it would be extra-special because it's the last place to be mentioned in the Hebrew Scriptures. But it's extra-extra-special for other reasons.

It's difficult to know what Beth Horon actually means. It could mean *house of the hollow* or *house of caves*. Often it's thought to be a reference to Horon, the so-called 'Valiant Shepherd', a deity worshipped by both Canaanites and Egyptians.[6] Or it could point to Horus, the falcon-god whose right eye was regarded as the sun. After all, even if Sheerah's grandfather Joseph worshipped the God of his forefathers—Abraham, Isaac and Jacob—her grandmother Asenath was the daughter of a priest of On. Since On was the centre of sun-worship, it might be an allusion to Horus.

On the other hand, Beth Horon may simply be *the white house*, from a Hebrew word for *white stuff*. The hillside of the twin towns is a limestone formation and, even today, elegant limestone houses are to be found there.[7] It also means *house of freedom* or *house of the free men*.[8]

Horon is a modern word for a *dance performed in ordered lines or circles* but it's unlikely that was its original meaning. However, the reverse is more than possible. Perhaps the name of the dance alludes back to Beth Horon. Its association with ordered lines is very strong and ancient.

The Talmud contains this proverb: *if two camels meet while on the ascent to Beth Horon, then they'll both fall if they try to ascend together, but they can go up safely if they proceed one after the other.*[9]

In other words: don't try to overtake on a steep and narrow path. It's dangerous. So be patient and orderly. The ascent of Beth Horon—the track between the lower and upper parts of the city—was a notorious incline that needed to be carefully negotiated one-by-one. The image of the single file necessary to climb the Ascent of Beth Horon was so compelling that the synagogue liturgy for Rosh Hashanah—the Jewish New Year, the 'birthday of the world'—compares all the inhabitants of the world passing before God and underneath His Shepherd's Rod to the orderly procession up that particular hillside.[10] Like sheep that a shepherd is checking, mankind is described as coming before God in single file on the Day of Judgment.[11]

Once we know this, Sheerah's genius as a town-planner and architect is evident. Remember she'd been born after her older brothers were killed stealing cattle. Her father was no longer a young man. Possibly she was the youngest in the family, almost an afterthought. Her grandfather may still have been alive but, if he was, he would have been very elderly by the time Sheerah was old enough to embark on her spree of civic construction. Even if he could have sent a squadron of soldiers to her aid in times of trouble, it's a long way from Egypt to Canaan. She therefore needed to fortify her cities and make them difficult to assault.

The strategic brilliance of her design for Beth Horon was that the half-city at the top of the ascent was easily defensible. A small band who knew the local terrain could protect the site against a large army. Like the three hundred Spartans who held off the might of the Persian army at the narrow pass of Thermopylae, the defenders of Beth Horon could pick off an entire battalion coming up the hillside in single file or in a narrow column with tight, compact rows. And that's exactly what the defenders did—more than once.

Isaiah refers to two major battles on the Ascent of Beth Horon that changed the course of Israelite history. If he'd lived another millennium, he'd have been able to add a few more to the tally.

> *The Lord will rise up as He did at Mount Perazim, He will rouse Himself as in the Valley of Gibeon—to do His work, His strange work, and perform His task, His alien task.*
>
> Isaiah 28:21 NIV

The battle at Mount Perazim was an attack by Philistine forces in a pincer movement aimed at Jerusalem. One flank of the enemy came up the valley below Jerusalem from the south, while the other moved in from the northwest. A third prong may have pushed in from the west. David's account of the battle seems to indicate that the forces coming up the valley from the south were swept away by a wall of water. A rout followed and the survivors fled, all the way to the Ascent of Beth Horon. There they were wiped out.

The second battle referred to in Isaiah 28:21 is the extraordinary victory of Sheerah's great-great-great-great-great-great-great-great-nephew,[12] Joshua, over a coalition of five kings. Once again, this took place on the Ascent of Beth Horon. As the Amorite armies fled up the hillside and the five kings found refuge in a cave, Joshua realised that the critical factor he needed was time. On that day:

> *Joshua spoke to the Lord in the presence of Israel: 'O sun, stand still over Gibeon, O moon, over the Valley of Aijalon.'*
>
> Joshua 10:12 BSB

This time-stopping event, when the sun and moon halted in their journey across the sky[13] and rocks fell out of heaven like missiles, is so unnatural that Isaiah refers to the miracle as God's *'strange work'* and *'alien task'*. Such an event is a sign, Isaiah says, that God will cancel the spiritual agreement the people had forged with the underworld to bring the forces of hell itself to protect the city of Jerusalem against the brutal Assyrian hordes. No way, said God.

Your covenant with death will be annulled.

Isaiah 28:18 ESV

The prophecy of an unnatural portent in the natural world points forward to the day Jesus died—when the ultimate annulment of a covenant with death took place. An 'eclipse' took place.

It was now about midday, but darkness came over the whole countryside until three in the afternoon, for there was an eclipse of the sun. The veil in the Temple sanctuary was split in two. Then Jesus gave a great cry and said, 'Father, into Your hands I commend My spirit.' And with these words, He died.

Luke 23:45–46 PHPS

Now, whatever caused this 'eclipse', it wasn't the moon. Because it was the Passover, the moon was in the worst possible position for a solar eclipse; and because it was daytime, it couldn't be a lunar eclipse either. This darkness was a truly abnormal phenomenon.

Isaiah's prophecy links the annulment of the covenant with death to the appointment of the Divine Cornerstone:

> *'See, I lay a stone in Zion,*
> *a tested stone,*
> *a precious cornerstone, a sure foundation;*
> *the one who believes will never be shaken.'*

Isaiah 28:16 BSB

Sheerah, like every city-builder of ancient times, would have laid down a cornerstone. Jesus Himself, the Chief Cornerstone, is the threshold, the foundation, upon which the living stones of His church are laid. Isaiah proclaimed the coming of Immanuel and deliberately linked the covenant-symbol of Sheerah's cities to that future event.

Now it might seem a little rash to suggest this was a purposeful connection on Isaiah's part. But it's not so far-fetched. The only other person in the Bible with *remnant* as part of the meaning of their name is Isaiah's son, Shear-Jashub, prophetically called *a remnant shall remain*. In addition, Isaiah makes a heavy emphasis throughout this passage on orders, lines, rows, single file and following in formation, planting in furrows, careful arrangements and regulations: the very thing that the Ascent of Beth Horon became renowned for in history, in liturgy and literature, and in a longstanding proverb about the flow of camel traffic.

> *Order on order, order on order, line on line, line on line, a little here, a little there.*

Isaiah 28:10 NASB

This is quickly repeated:

> *Order on order, order on order, line on line, line on line, a little here, a little there.*

Isaiah 28:13 NASB

And then, in what seems to be a mixed metaphor, Isaiah turns to an extended sequence of farming imagery, describing at one point the work of a ploughman:

He plants wheat in rows and barley in plots, and rye within its border.

Isaiah 28:25 BSB

Now that word for *rows* in that verse is 'shurah', followed immediately by *barley*, 'sheorah'. Both of these look like puns on the name of Sheerah. I think Isaiah employed the agricultural metaphor just so he could hint at Sheerah's name as well as the discipline required for successful negotiation of the path between her cities. In doing so, he was repeating his reminder to the people of Jerusalem about God's covenant defence and His miraculous intervention in the past on those very slopes.

Now Isaiah couldn't know that, centuries after his time, other significant battles would be fought—with equally spectacular results—on the Ascent of Beth Horon. In the year 66, Jewish rebels won a stunning victory here. They wiped out the equivalent of an entire legion with missile fire and volleys of arrows, reminiscent of the stones falling from heaven back in Joshua's day.

Perhaps that image of the armies of heaven fighting against five ancient kings was what encouraged the people of Judea to support a full-scale war with Rome. The result was disastrous—the Temple destroyed and ransacked—yet the initial enthusiasm is perfectly understandable. After all, the opening win at Beth Horon would have evoked Joshua's defeat of the Amorites as well as David's victory over the Philistines. In addition, in popular imagination it would also have called to mind the triumph of the Maccabees against the Greek overlords some 232 years previously. The Maccabees too found their first flush of success on the Ascent of Beth Horon.

But Sheerah's work, as Isaiah signposted for us, involves the long game of God. She's unutterably different from Cain, the first murderer, or from Nimrod, the traditional builder of the Tower of Babel and reputedly the world's first totalitarian dictator.

She was appointed, as the first city-builder in Israel, to set in place the blueprint for an ideal city. She was the creator of a new prototype—one whose hidden potential would only be realised in the ages to come.

Hers would be a city where time stood still.

Hers would be a city of first and last things.

Hers would be a city defended by the angel armies of heaven.

Hers would be a city whose very stones cried out, testifying of its covenantal form.

Hers would be a city that points to the ultimate City—the New Jerusalem—and whose civic body images a spiritual Body.

Hers would be a city designed to prophesy of the new covenant of Jesus.

Sheerah's third city, Uzzen-Sheerah, means *listen to Sheerah*. The name is thought to be essentially a prayer: an appeal to God, asking Him to listen to her. Cain named his city after his son, but Sheerah named one after herself.

Yet she named it in a way that invokes a *house of prayer*, thus foreshadowing the prophecy of Isaiah 56:7 NKJV regarding the Temple:

My house shall be called a house of prayer for all nations.

The comparison between Sheerah and the better-known city-builders, Cain and Nimrod, could hardly be greater. In contrast to rebellious Babel, her cities were about covenant. In contrast to Babylon, the mother of harlots, Beth Horon was to be repeatedly associated with fidelity of God. The first time we see this in operation it's when Joshua keeps covenant with the Gibeonites, while God keeps covenant with him at the same time as He's annulling a covenant with Death. Just think: squadron files and army columns are very orderly constructions. However, just as God turned the systemic arrangement of language into confusion at Babel, He turned order into disorder when He cancelled a covenant with Death.

Beth Horon still exists today. It's still in two parts: Beit Ur-al Fauqa and Beit Ur-al Tahta. The Ascent has been tamed by a multi-lane highway.

Yet as we look back to its founder, we see she was a visionary, bequeathing a heritage to future generations.

Much more than building a city, Sheerah built a legacy for the future. God may not be calling you to build a city, but He's definitely calling you to build a legacy.

I'd always wanted to write books. But, whenever I entered a bookstore, I'd be overwhelmed with discouragement. I'd look at the shelves and say to myself: 'What makes me think the world needs my book added to all this?' This, along with many rejections, meant I'd sometimes find myself in a tar pit of lost hope.

Then I discovered the wonderfully rollicking medieval poem, *Sir Gawain and the Green Knight*. It took me several years to understand its mathematical design and, in the process, I came to appreciate it would have taken decades to put together—to marry up specific ideas with particular line numbers and to wrangle it so it seems like an effortless romp, rather than a stodgy lesson.

I also realised that, just at the time the author would have finished his life's grand work, the hierarchy of the English church forbade the publication of theological writings in the vernacular.[14] *Sir Gawain and the Green Knight* might not sound like a treatise in theology but, truly, it *is*. I couldn't imagine the crushed heartbreak of someone who spent decades perfecting and polishing this gem of literature only to find it was forbidden to seek an audience for it. I'd have been unbelievably depressed and disillusioned to find my effort was wasted.

And yet...

The author couldn't have known his work was not for his time. It was for half a millennia in the future—to inspire some of the greatest Christian authors of the twentieth century. And with that realisation, I wondered: *what if my writing is not for my time? What if it's for the future?*

And so I persevered.

What if, like Sheerah and the author of *Sir Gawain and the Green Knight*, your calling is not for your lifetime? Are you still willing to do it?

Yes?

Then now is the perfect time to ask the Lord where to start.

Prayer for myself

Heavenly Father,

I can only fall on my knees and beg your forgiveness for my lack of motivation—for my casual attitude towards You and the tasks You have set before me. You created me anew in Christ Jesus and appointed me to undertake good works that You prepared beforehand for me to accomplish.

Sheerah is a truly inspirational model. With close to nothing she achieved what seems to me to be nearly impossible. I am reminded of the words of Jesus: *'All things are possible for one who believes.'*

What a blessing Sheerah was. What a monument and memorial she left behind as a template for women through all the ages to emulate. Thank you, Sheerah. Thank You, Father God, for Sheerah. She did what needed doing to get the job done—no excuses, no whinging, no whining—just a lot of get up and go, and on with the job.

O Father, how different from Sheerah I have been. I repent, Father, of believing I simply could not do a lot of the tasks You asked of me. I was sincere but I was also sincerely mistaken. It was true I couldn't do those tasks in my own strength, but I recognise that You were never asking me to do them in my own strength.

I've come to believe the lies of the enemy: the lies that said I'm incapable, I'm unworthy, I'm incompetent, I'm unqualified.

I ask you to change my heart. I am not Sheerah and can never be her. Still I ask that You motivate me to be **like** her so that in future I will say, 'Yes, Lord. *Yes*, Lord! *Yes*. I am willing and, with Your help, there is nothing that we cannot together achieve.'

I ask this is the name of Jesus of Nazareth. Amen

Prayer for others

Father of all, may I honour You in all I ask for my friends and loved ones. Father, the pathway between the two cities that Sheerah built on the Ascent of Beth Horon reminds me of the narrow way into life that Your Son, Jesus, spoke of. 'Few there be that find it,' He said.

Yet I know with the help of Jesus we can find it. So I call on You, Father God, for Your mercy and guidance. May the Holy Spirit give direction and wisdom to my friends who struggle to choose that narrow way, struggle to keep on it, struggle to find their path back to it, struggle to stay in that timeless place with You as Immanuel, *God with us*. Instead of allowing You to battle on our behalf, we feel the need to do it all in our own strength.

Lord, my friends know You and they know that You have a special role for them in Your kingdom. Some of them are builders, 'city-builders' in the sense that You want them to take Your blueprints for the advancement of Your City and bring them to pass. Yet they are still to discover what Your plan is and how they fit into it. Help them, Father, and where necessary, help me to help them. My friends are willing and they, like me, are able—not in their own strength but in Yours—however they lack the spirit of Sheerah which was guided and underpinned by the Holy Spirit.

Holy Spirit, I ask You to overshadow my friends in all they think and do and say, so that heaven and earth meet together and You are glorified.

Father, as I ask this for my friends I realise that I also need the same mercy and grace I ask for them. Teach us how to change and to seek Your guidance earlier.

Father, I ask also that, as we reach towards You at a deeper level, our trust in You will be strengthened, deepened and enriched as we are touched by You at a new level.

May we all have a thankful heart to know Your peace, love, grace and truth in our lives—renewed in our mind as we are being transformed into the image of Jesus.

Thank You, Father. Thank You, Jesus. Thank You, Holy Spirit.

In the name of Jesus of Nazareth, the Way, the Truth and the Life. Amen.

2
Woman and Mother: Nation-Shaper

2
Woman and Mother: Nation-Shaper

TWELVE WOMEN APPEAR IN the first two chapters of Exodus: two midwives, the mother and sister of Moses, Pharaoh's daughter and then the seven daughters of a priest of Midian. We might not know much about many of them but, truth be told, we don't know much about seven of Jacob's twelve sons either. The bit-parts of Asher and Issachar, Naphtali and Zebulon, Dan, Gad and even Benjamin in the stories of the patriarchs are non-speaking background roles. If ever they featured in the narrative, most of their storyline got lost on the cutting-room floor.

We may think women got a raw deal when it came to recording their names, let alone their deeds, in the long march of salvation history. It's true, they did. But then so did anyone who was not the designated hero of the moment. The well-known biblical stories present us with champions so obvious and flashy that it's easy to overlook the quiet and unexpected ones.

The fifth of the twelve women introduced in the opening of Exodus is Pharaoh's daughter. We don't ever learn the name she was given in the royal house of Egypt, though later in Scripture we're told what she was called amongst the Hebrews.

Moses is the number one hero of the Exodus story. He's the law-giver and leader who fronted Pharaoh and spoke the word of the Lord: *'Let My people go!'*

But without the actions of his adoptive mother, there would not have been a Moses to deliver the people of Israel. Without her small spur-of-the-moment decision on which the hinge of history swung, Moses the hero might not ever have existed so that God could call on him to rescue the people.

Pharaoh's daughter was not an Israelite. She was an Egyptian princess, a citizen of the mightiest power on earth and the daughter of its king. Egypt was at its peak and was pre-eminent among the nations. Her father, however, became aware of a potential peril within his own kingdom: a racially distinct people who held an enclave in his land. They'd been there for centuries but their loyalty was questionable simply because they were 'other'. The Hebrews therefore posed a political threat.

In an attempt to control their population, the Pharaoh ordered his subjects to throw Hebrew babies into the River Nile. Then…

…one day his daughter, accompanied by her servants, went down the Nile to take a bath. A basket bobbing in the reeds caught her attention. A baby was crying. A servant brought the basket to her. And there, inside, was a Hebrew boy—one of the infants her father wanted to kill.

In that split second, she could have simply overturned the basket and let the child drown. Or she could have directed one of the servants to fling the child out into the deep water. But she did not.

She had compassion.

And then a stranger approached her, a young girl who asked, 'Do you want me to find a Hebrew mother to feed the baby?'

Pharaoh's daughter must have suspected who the girl was, even as she said yes. She'd grown up in a court rife with political intrigue, after all. Yet not only did she decide to rescue a child of the people her father had designated as an enemy, she paid the biological mother to feed and nurse her own baby. Her compassion was not a passing phase or a temporary whim—she went as far as naming the boy and adopting him as her own child.

The princess made a choice to go against everything her father valued. She made a stand against her nation. She drew a line in the sand and positioned herself in defiance of every Egyptian who'd killed an Israelite child. She is the only person recorded as acting against her father's will. What may have started as an instinctive reaction to the needs of a crying child became deliberate in action and full of thoughtful planning. Not only did Pharaoh's daughter adopt Moses as her own child and pay a Hebrew woman to feed him, she risked absolutely everything she had for his sake.

Palace intrigue being what it was, the chances a servant would inform her father of her small rebellious act were probably high. Even if her servants were utterly loyal to her, sooner or later it would be obvious that a toddler had mysteriously appeared where there was none before. So Pharaoh's daughter not only risked her life but parental favour as well. She could have lost everything.

However she decided to have compassion and made a righteous decision to rescue the baby. She turned her back on her father's abusive behavior. She knew his decrees. She knew that, back when he'd been enthroned as Pharaoh, one who did not know Joseph—the vizier of an earlier generation—he had not accepted the covenant friendship between the Egyptians and Israelites. Instead when he rose to power, he decided to eliminate normal life for the people of Israel. His language was splashed with degrading propaganda, portraying the Israelites as animals and insects—in effect, attempting to legitimise his brutal treatment.

He dehumanised them. Not only that, he accused them of conspiracy and treachery, telling his own people that the Israelites were an 'enemy within' who would aid the 'enemy without' as soon as an opportunity presented itself. This lie provided the justification for reducing the Jewish people into slavery. They had to go out and make bricks and build store houses for the Egyptians.

The situation worsened as the Israelite population continued to grow and multiply. This was the point at which Pharaoh, unhappy and determined to be in control, encouraged the Egyptians to throw the Hebrew babies into the Nile. He'd also ordered the midwives to crush the heads of newborns on the birthing stone. In short, Pharaoh had become very vicious and violent towards the Israelites.

Yet his daughter had a completely different mindset. She was adamantly against abuse. And so she rescued one child—she could not rescue all of them, but she could rescue one.

The Israelite slave boy she saved would be adopted as a royal prince and would grow up, having the best education, the best food, the safest place. He may have been bullied—and perhaps that was the source of his speech impediment—but he was far better off than in the slave pits. The opposition of Pharaoh's daughter to the systemic abuse of her father is displayed in the character of Moses—as an adult, the first we see of him is when he overreacts to an Egyptian overseer beating a Hebrew slave.

Pharaoh's daughter took risks on her son's behalf, remaining committed to his welfare through the long years of his upbringing. She took responsibility for him and, in doing so, demonstrated courage of the highest order.

Amazingly, we know him by the name she gave him. Not by the name that Jochebed and Amram gave him. In the Torah, parents generally name their children although, in the case of special individuals, God Himself performs the naming. For example, El Shaddai told Abraham and Sarah to call the long-promised son 'Isaac', and the Angel of the Lord pronounced 'Israel' over Jacob in his renaming. God Himself changed the names of Abram and Sarai to Abraham and Sarah. And although the Pharaoh of the famine era called his trusted vizier 'Zaphenath-Paneah', we still know him as Joseph. Hebrew names predominate throughout Scripture.

So, it is remarkable that the hero of the Exodus, the greatest of the prophets, the deliverer of Israel is universally known by the name given to him by his adoptive mother! Moses, she called him, because she said, *'I drew him from the water.'*

Moses may have had many names. It is said he was known by ten different names during his lifetime.[15] Nevertheless the name he has been invariably called throughout the ages is 'Moses' which had overtones in the Egyptian language of *child of the river-god* or *son of the Nile*[16] but in Hebrew is a prophetic forth-telling: the one who was drawn out of water would be the means of drawing the Israelite nation out of water—the waters of the Red Sea.[17]

God Himself honours the name that Pharaoh's daughter chose and, instead of calling him by a Hebrew name, continues to use 'Moses'.[18] That is amazing. Because He wants to declare that what Pharaoh's daughter has done is very significant and righteous in His eyes, He ratifies her choice. Even though she grew up in an environment where abuse was commonplace, she stood up to it and modeled courage and perseverance for her adopted son. Her character reflected that of almighty God: compassionate, faithful, merciful and kind. When God descended in a cloud and passed in front of Moses on Mount Sinai, He announced concerning Himself:

> *The Lord, the Lord God, merciful and gracious, longsuffering, and abundant in goodness and truth.*
>
> Exodus 34:6 KJV

We can know for sure that Pharaoh's daughter was indeed just like this because Scripture records a truly astonishing name for her. 1 Chronicles 4:18 reveals that she became one of those foreigners who, like Zipporah, Ruth and

Rahab, covenantally joined themselves to the Hebrew nation through marriage.[19] Amongst the Jewish people she was called Bithiah, meaning *daughter of God*.[20]

Like Abram becoming Abraham, Jacob becoming Israel and Simon becoming Peter, the 'daughter of Pharaoh' became the 'daughter of God'.

Why did God give her a new name? Because names reflect both identity and destiny. God tells us through the name Bithiah that she does not share the values and character of her earthly father, but those of her heavenly Father. Pharaoh was sadistic, pitiless, cold and cruel but, despite her upbringing and despite knowing the rules and expectations of her father, she has the moral courage to defy the abuser. She is God's architect for a nation yet unborn. She models the goodness, kindness and faithfulness needed to shape the messiah who foreshadows the Messiah. Moses could have turned against his people, forsaken his blood heritage and moulded himself to the ways of his adopted grandfather. But he follows his foster mother instead—who, although she does not know Yahweh of Israel, still finds His embers of love in her heart and fans those flames with her actions.

So—who knows how many decades later?—God gave her a name which means *you're My daughter, you have My character and you steward My values*.

Moral courage like this is best seen as a gleaming jewel in the heart of darkness. The nation-forgers and architects of national deliverance are not always the ones out front; sometimes they are simply those who, at a moment of critical choice, opt for the good and the true and the righteous.

During the Nazi occupation of Austria prior to World War II, a quarter of a million people cheered Adolf Hitler at a huge rally in Vienna. In the middle of the crowds that day, as other Jews were being rounded up and forced to clean pavements and toilets, a young girl, Lilith-Sylvia Doron, met the Chinese ambassador. Dr Ho Fengshan knew her family. He made the decision to accompany her home. 'He claimed that, thanks to his diplomatic status, the [Nazis] would not dare harm us as long as he remained in our home,' she said. 'Ho continued to visit our home on a permanent basis to protect us from the Nazis.'

'Seeing the Jews so doomed,' Dr Ho wrote in his memoir, 'it was only natural to feel deep compassion, and from a humanitarian standpoint, to be impelled to help them.'

Only natural, Dr Ho wrote. Yet history testifies that it is not natural to choose compassion. Dr Ho went on to risk his life and career as he organised the rescue of thousands of Jews, helping them escape the horror of Nazi extermination machine. As midnight approached in Hitler's reign of terror, he was one of the few candles burning brightly.

The basic core values of humanity are compassion and faithfulness. Together with courage, they inspire us to greatness. These values are truly universal, I believe, because whether you have religion or not, whether you have faith or not, each one of us as a human has, at the fundamental core of our being, a spark of kindness and courage. We can allow that spark to be kindled to a flame or we can snuff it out. That's our choice.

In Israel, the Holocaust Memorial Museum has many areas dedicated to the righteous Gentiles—Dr Ho Fengshan amongst them. Like Pharaoh's daughter, they are a supreme symbol of what it means for humanity to be an image-bearer of God. In risking their lives, they saved lives and changed the course of history. They defied abuse and evil; they stood against inhumanity; they rebelled against hatred and exploitation.

One of the rabbinic sages drew a striking lesson from Bithiah's story. God said to her, 'Moses was not your son, yet you called him your son. You are not My daughter, but I shall call you: "My daughter."'

When you are struggling with your identity and your place in God's Kingdom, remember the story of Bithiah—the woman who changed the course of nations.

Prayer for myself

Heavenly Father, thank You for the example of Bithiah. Thank you for that moment of compassion that became a lifetime of courage. Please mould me and shape me and recreate me anew so that, like Bithiah, I will have the moral boldness to stand for what is right in a world where it is often politically incorrect to do so.

Father, I repent of the many times I have looked the other way when faced with difficult decisions. Father, our cruel and sadistic laws are very little different from those of Pharaoh's time and I feel so helpless to help those who are genuinely helpless. But, in reality, I am no less helpless than Bithiah was when she stood and chose life for one little boy. In choosing tenderness and compassion Bithiah's actions changed the course of history. Like Joseph, but in a different way, she was the preserver of a nation. So let it be also with me, Lord—in whatever different way You want me to work.

Bithiah was a princess and a daughter of a king. So am I. I am Your princess and the daughter of the King of Heaven. Lord, whenever I think I am unable and it is too hard to do anything in the political, civil or legal sphere, remind me that You are my heavenly Father and, with You at my side, all things are possible.

Bithiah counted it more important to be Your daughter and side with You than with her earthly father and political master. Lord, when I am afraid of the consequences of standing up for the helpless, remind me of her choice. Empower me to choose as she did.

Remind me too, Father, that when I do something good today I may never see the results in this lifetime. However, the good will continue to flow down through the generational stream to many and for the healing of Your people.

I ask this in the name of Jesus of Nazareth. Amen.

Prayer for others

Heavenly Father, Creator of all,

I pray that Your Holy Spirit will encourage my friends, colleagues and loved ones to join the 'Bithiah club'. I pray, Lord, that if necessary they will be the foundation members of a new group in the area where they live. Three or four people standing together for righteousness. Yes, Lord, that is all it takes. Three or four people with a quiet and steadfast passion for truth can change families, churches, streets, suburbs, cities and nations when we turn to You in humility, commitment and love. When we cherish life from pre-birth to the grave we can change the world in the way Bithiah did when she honoured the life of the baby she found hidden in the waters.

I pray this for my friends and for myself. I pray for the courage to stand up and stand out, to speak up and speak out, when it's needed. I pray that we will become alert to the techniques of shut up and shutdown used to silence those who want to give a voice to the voiceless and help to the helpless.

I pray also that we will work to create an intentional culture of honour so that You are respected, Your glory is made visible, and the betterment of Your people results. We may be unable to change the entire world but we can change our own small corner. May we do this, Lord, with a right heart and a right spirit. May we be always aware we are a signpost to You in the world in whatever we say and do.

I join with my friends and commit to pray, to cherish life, to respect and honour You and each other. I do this in the same of Your beloved Son, Jesus of Nazareth. Amen.

3
Woman and Mother: Paradigm-Shifters

3
Woman and Mother: Paradigm-Shifters

Scripture has a definite 'thing' about groups of five women.

Exodus, the second book in the Torah, opens with the exploits of five women who are instrumental in saving the life of Moses. Numbers, the second last book of the Torah, ends with five women creating a new precedent for inheritance. Yes, five again—arranged in basically the same position at both the front and back of the Torah.

Something very similar exists in the gospels. The first chapter of Matthew mentions five women within the genealogy of Jesus—though obviously there had to have been a lot more! And, although the information is scattered and the exact number of women who made their way to the tomb and were witnesses to the resurrection of Jesus is uncertain, the most likely answer appears to be five.[21]

Importantly, the majority of these women are named. They are not anonymous. Back in Exodus, the first of these notable women are the midwives, Shiphrah and Puah. After them comes the mother and sister of Moses who are initially unnamed before being revealed as Jochebed and Miriam. Lastly there's Pharaoh's daughter whose identity is never unveiled in any of the five books of the Torah but is only named as Bithiah in the genealogical record of Chronicles.

Moving forward, Matthew's gospel lists Tamar, Rahab, Ruth, and then rather strangely 'Uriah's wife' instead of Bathsheba, and lastly, Mary the mother of Jesus. Perhaps Matthew wanted to reflect the first chapter of Exodus and hint that his gospel was the record of a nation-changing event of a similar order. His subtle way of doing this was not just choosing to mention five and only five women but also, by saying 'Uriah's wife', he was making use of the same kind of veiling that hid the name of Pharaoh's daughter.

The account of the resurrection is either the last, or close to the last, event mentioned in any gospel. By combining the information in the varying reports, we can conclude that there were probably five women who took spices to the tomb of Jesus on the morning of the resurrection: Mary Magdalene, Mary the mother of James, Salome, Joanna and at least one unnamed other.

Seriously, this business of five women is an important motif in Scripture. Jesus likens the kingdom of heaven to five wise virgins and five foolish ones who are waiting up for the Bridegroom. Perhaps this parable is in some way connected to the five handmaidens of Abigail who accompanied her when she went to become David's wife.

There are still further sets of five females. Although there were many women who prophesied and whose names are given in the biblical record, there are only five who are actually designated as prophets, at least in the Hebrew portion of the Scriptures: these are Miriam, Deborah, Huldah, Noadiah and 'the prophetess' who was married to Isaiah. Likewise, there are five barren women who eventually gave birth and who are mentioned there: Sarah, Rebekah, Rachel, Hannah and the wife of Manoah who was also the mother of Samson.[22]

There's something mysterious about 'five women' that runs like a grace-thread through the Bible. And despite the fact I don't know what the significance of these groups could possibly be in God's eyes, I'm still going to have a go at scratching the surface of the symbolism to see what we can find.

Now the only time any of these groups of five women are all named up front and together is in the last chapter of the book of Numbers. Here the daughters of the grandson of the first cousin of Sheerah—yes, Sheerah the city-builder—are mentioned.[23] This first cousin's grandson was Zelophehad and he had no sons—just five daughters: Mahlah, No'ah, Hoglah, Milkah and Tirzah.

Poor Mahlah—her name seems to mean *disease*. It's probable she was born when Zelophehad was sick but it's unfortunate she had to be a constant reminder of that situation. It's as unpleasant as Jabez who, through his name, was a lifetime memorial to the anguish he caused his mother in childbirth. Jabez means *pain, persecution* and *walled in*—so it's no wonder he prayed neither to give nor receive pain and also for his territory to be expanded.

No'ah does little better than her older sister—her name means *shaking* or *wandering*. Keeping to the same theme, Hoglah is along the lines of *wobble, hobble* or *hop*. It's thought that perhaps her name might refer to a *partridge*. But perhaps it simply meant her father's disease had progressed from shaking to wobbling.

The last two daughters fare considerably better. So perhaps Zelophehad was recovering from the shakes and wobbles by the time Milkah was born because she was named *queen*, or *counsel*. And the last, Tirzah, is named for *delight, pleasure, beauty*.

Zelophehad's own name is suggestive of *firstborn* or perhaps means *shadow of the fear*.[24] We don't know anything about him other than he was a descendant of Joseph, he had five daughters but no sons, and he died.

So then:

> *One day a petition was presented by the daughters of Zelophehad—Mahlah, No'ah, Hoglah, Milcah, and Tirzah. Their father, Zelophehad, was a descendant of Hepher son of Gilead, son of Makir, son of Manasseh, son of Joseph. These women stood before Moses, Eleazar the priest, the tribal leaders, and the entire community at the entrance of the Tabernacle.*
>
> *'Our father died in the wilderness,' they said. 'He was not among Korah's followers, who rebelled against the Lord; he died because of his own sin. But he had no sons. Why should the name of our father disappear from his clan just because he had no sons? Give us property along with the rest of our relatives.'*
>
> *So Moses brought their case before the Lord.*
>
> Numbers 27:1–5 NLT

This is a faith-inspired request, if ever there was one! The division of inheritance is quite abstract at this point. There is no specific land the five daughters can point to and say, 'We want *that*, there.' They believe, however, that God will fulfill His promise to His people and they don't want their family to be sidelined. They want to be included as heirs to His promise and they're prepared to make their claim.

Now in the first book in this series, *More Precious than Pearls*, the heroic role of the women—the mothers in Israel—during the forty years of the desert wanderings has been extensively explored. The daughters of Zelophehad don't represent some sudden emergence of strong, assertive women who are prepared to stand their ground against a repressive patriarchal society. They demonstrate a powerful continuity with their firm and fearless sisters and mothers.

The women of the wilderness years have long been regarded as rock-solid pillars of the faith by rabbinic thinkers and commentators. The Jewish sages see subtle nuances in the text that proclaim these women as maintaining steadfast loyalty to God in the face of the unnerving and wavering idolatry of their menfolk.

For many Jewish writers, Moses might be the deliverer and the law-giver, nevertheless the real heroes of the Exodus story are the mothers of Israel. It's a shock to read some rabbinic commentaries—and to be surprised at the differences in interpretation of the Hebrew text. Who would imagine, reading a Christian Bible, that the women camped at Mount Sinai refused to give up their gold jewelry for the making of the golden calf? Or that they were then the first to offer it for the ornamentation of the Tabernacle?

I often wonder if our translators have projected the Greco-Roman world's hatred of women back into the culture of the Bible. Instead of seeing the daughters of Zelophehad as part of an environment where courage was so commonplace for women it virtually faded into the background, they are seen as bold and daring. In a sense, it's true that they were brave in challenging the status quo. However it's also very important to see that they were part of a society where women were used to drawing a line in the sand and telling the men, 'Enough!' There was no guarantee they'd be listened to, but they'd had womanly chutzpah modeled to them for years.

And so the daughters of Zelophehad had the audacity to front up to Moses and to basically tell the men to ask God whether the rules of inheritance were fair or not. It's interesting to note that these five women didn't feel the need to call in a male sponsor. They had the confidence to advocate and campaign on their own behalf. At the actual time they were asking, the distribution of land had not taken place—in fact, it was the best part of a decade in the future. So whatever way the ruling went wouldn't immediately affect them. Yet they had their eyes on what was yet-to-come.

Were they ruled by FOMO—**f**ear **o**f **m**issing **o**ut? I suspect not. Certainly, for some people today, FOMO is an almost obsessive worry. They see other people apparently being favoured and blessed more than they are, and so they complain in private. Bitter little monologues take up far too much mental real estate. But they are unwilling to take any risk and speak their thoughts in public. They are reluctant to do what the daughters of Zelophehad did: stand up and make a case for justice.

> *And the Lord replied to Moses, 'The claim of the daughters of Zelophehad is legitimate. You must give them a grant of land along with their father's relatives. Assign them the property that would have been given to their father.*
>
> *'And give the following instructions to the people of Israel: If a man dies and has no son, then give his inheritance to his daughters. And if he has no daughter either, transfer his inheritance to his brothers. If he has no brothers, give his inheritance to his father's brothers. But if his father has no brothers, give his inheritance to the nearest relative in his clan. This is a legal requirement for the people of Israel, just as the Lord commanded Moses.'*
>
> Numbers 27:6–11 NLT

Remarkably, the ruling sought by the daughters of Zelophehad wasn't an exception that applied only to themselves. They set a legal precedent. Their advocacy changed the law regarding inheritance—where there was no male heir, the line of posterity could pass through any females.

Now some of their relatives who were also descendants of Joseph foresaw potential problems with this ruling if the daughters of Zelophehad chose to marry outside their own tribal unit:

> *When the Year of Jubilee for the Israelites comes, their inheritance will be added to that of the tribe into which they marry, and their property will be taken from the tribal inheritance of our ancestors.*
>
> Numbers 36:4 NIV

So they asked for a modification to ensure an inheritance could not pass from one tribe to another. The Lord therefore amended His ruling for the daughters of Zelophehad with this proviso:

> *They may marry anyone they please as long as they marry within their father's tribal clan. No inheritance in Israel is to pass from one tribe to another, for every Israelite shall keep the tribal inheritance of their ancestors.*
>
> Numbers 36:6–7 NIV

The men didn't seek to overturn the Lord's command, just to prevent a future difficulty. The precedent created by the daughters of Zelophehad was not upended or set aside, it simply had some boundaries placed upon it.

Mahlah, No'ah, Hoglah, Milkah and Tirzah were willing to place themselves under authority and keep the ruling given to them. They married their cousins on their father's side.

Their story shows that they were architects of a paradigm shift. They ushered in carefully considered new rules for inheritance of land that preserved clan justice but allowed the inflow of natural justice for orphaned women.

Another extraordinary paradigm shift occurs in the gospels. The witnesses to the resurrection, as every gospel writer notes, are women: Mary Magdalene, Mary the mother of James, Salome, Joanna and one other.

At that time in the first century, women could not testify in a court of law. Yet God chose them as His witnesses to the most wondrous event in salvation history: the precedent above and beyond all other precedents—the conquering of Death, and the spectacular return of Jesus from the grave.

When it comes to the creation of precedents and the shifting of paradigms, God sometimes wants us to participate with Him when He says:

Behold, I am doing a new thing; now it springs forth, do you not perceive it?

Isaiah 43:19 ESV

But we can't just run with what we want. Just as He acceded to the request of the daughters of Zelophehad and then placed restrictions so that the new ruling fit with the old, not displaced it or created chaos within it, so too the precedents He wants us to create must not undermine His Word. Or introduce new inequality to rectify old injustice.

We must ring in fairness, bring in integrity, swing in impartiality, wing in righteousness. The new Eden is a garden with a tree whose leaves are for the healing of the nations. The fruit of that tree is love, joy, peace, patience, kindness, goodness, faithfulness, gentleness, self-control. This new Eden is the inheritance of those called to be heirs in His kingdom—and, as heirs, stewards and keepers of it all. Let us sing with Him over it:

Sing about a fruitful vineyard.
I, the Lord, am its keeper;
I water it continually.
I guard it night and day.

Isaiah 27:2 BSB

So let us also step into the inheritance the daughters of Zelophehad won for all the heirs of the divine covenant—both the natural descendents of Abraham and and those who, by faith, have been grafted in to the Family of God.

Prayer for myself

Abba Father, sometimes I feel left out. No, that's not true. *Often* I feel left out. My heart cries, 'That's so unfair!' but my mouth clamps shut. I can't bring myself to ask, 'What about me?' All because whenever I've asked my parents, my teachers, my boss—everyone who represents authority—in the past, my heart has been trampled on and my soul bruised.

Forgive me, Father, for becoming a coward. I want to stand up against injustice and ask for my rights—for what *is* genuinely right. But I don't. At the time, I think I'm unable but the truth is I'm weak-willed. I lack the courage and ability to stand firm for what is mine. I lie to myself. I say, 'It doesn't matter,' which soon becomes: '*I* don't matter.' Or I say, 'It doesn't hurt,' which is only one step away from '*I* don't hurt.'

Lord, it does matter and it does hurt.

Lord, You are the Good Shepherd. You went out to find the one lamb who was lost and missing out. You changed the laws of inheritance, just because Mahlah, No'ah, Hoglah, Milkah and Tirzah asked not to miss out. And when they asked for their case to be put to You, You codified forever the rights of women to inherit.

Forgive me, Father, for the times I've been silent. I thought it was about *me*—and it was, but it was not just about me. I could have changed the future if I'd dared speak. So, cause me to be like the great-granddaughters of Sheerah's first cousin. There must have been something about that family, Lord. They had backbone. Something about those women—they were not timid wimps. They were feisty and had a sense of fairness.

But their desire for fairness didn't mean they smashed through boundaries and created injustice within their clan, just so they could receive the fairness due to them. They were women of grace! Lord, alert me when I might be insisting on discrimination against others in order to receive justice for myself. Cause me to be a woman of grace!

One other thing about these five women, Lord—they stood firm and together. They stood before Moses and the entire assembly. They presented their request and eventually their desires were granted. O Lord, empower me to be like them.

Father, I repent of making excuses for my lack of determination and courage to face authority. Forgive me, and strengthen my resolve. Teach me, Father, what it means to be a person of integrity, honesty and boldness and, in becoming so, may I become a Kingdom-Builder and Paradigm-Shifter to help You bring heaven to earth in my small corner.

I ask to be one who challenges and changes unfair, unjust laws. I ask Your wisdom to usher in fairness in every form in my community so that no one is left out.

I ask all this in Jesus' name. Amen.

Prayer for others

Father in heaven, who sees all and hears our pleas with justice and compassion, I ask that my sisters will be bold, but not too bold. I ask that they will not cower in fear but step forward in courage to call for exceptions—not to privilege some and thus disadvantage others, but to usher in fairness for all. I ask that my sisters will hear and heed Your instructions to us in the sure knowledge that You will never lead us into danger or send us astray. Give us ears to hear, Father, and a heart to understand.

Lord, I pray for my sisters—I pray You speak to their hearts in ways that we understand so that, together with You, we can renew the face of this earth and create a Kingdom of justice, mercy and compassion.

Holy Spirit, come with Your strength and power in exactly the way each of us needs so that together we are a formidable powerhouse for good. May the Fruit of the Spirit be evident in our lives: love, joy, peace, patience, kindness, goodness, faithfulness, gentleness, self-control. And let us never lose sight of who You are and that You are the glue that binds us together in love.

I pray also, Father, for our brothers in Christ. I pray that my sisters and I will first of all respect and honour You in all that we say and do and think, and then honour our brothers too. I pray that we never lose sight of the fact that, in our families, we are a signpost to Your kingdom of love, compassion, justice and mercy which is often the only sign of You that many ever see.

I ask all this in the holy name of Jesus Christ who died to give us life. Amen.

4
Woman and Mother: Chamberlain

4
Woman and Mother: Chamberlain

An army cannot move beyond its supply lines. Well, it can—but it will soon have to retreat.

One of the greatest generals of World War II was the German commander, Erwin Rommel. A sly and aggressive tactician, he demonstrated considerable skill at *blitzkrieg*—an innovative manoeuvre dubbed *lightning war*. His victories made him famous and popular.

When he was sent to North Africa, he rapidly acquired the nickname 'The Desert Fox' for his wily strategies and stunning victories. Despite his brilliance, he had a singular blind-spot. Throughout his career, it was evident that logistical planning was not his strong point. He'd gain massive ground only to lose it again because he'd moved so far beyond his supply lines that food, water and armaments could not reach his advanced position.

Back during World War I, the same issue had faced the British and Commonwealth forces as they advanced into the Holy Land. How could they keep the troops supplied? In the quiet of the desert, trucks or planes would easily be spotted by the enemy and picked off with ease. Even a boat cruising up the coast to a designated rendezvous would give away its position by the sound of its engine.

The solution was provided by those Commonwealth soldiers who'd enlisted and come from the Pacific Islands—sailors who'd answered the call to war from Rarotonga, Polynesia and other parts of Oceania. These were men who didn't need electronic equipment to know where they were: they could navigate by the stars. These were men who didn't need an engine to power a boat: they could utilise the wind and the currents. These were men who didn't need a big crew or a big vessel to transport a hefty load: they knew how to build a craft then virtually unheard of—the catamaran.

The liberation of the Holy Land from centuries of Ottoman rule was only possible because the men of the Pacific ensured the Allied supply lines kept pace with their victories. They were purveyors—those who delivered and furnished the needs of an army on the move. Their role was crucial but also all too often overlooked.

The purveyors of Scripture—the providers, provisioners, bursars and pursers—are often women. Their role was also crucial but again it is all too often overlooked.

> *Jesus traveled about from one town and village to another, proclaiming the good news of the kingdom of God. The Twelve were with Him, and also some women who had been cured of evil spirits and diseases: Mary (called Magdalene) from whom seven demons had come out; Joanna the wife of Chuza, the manager of Herod's*

> *household; Susanna; and many others. These women were helping to support them out of their own means.*
>
> Luke 8:1–3 NIV

These women were not simply supporters of Jesus and His band of disciples, they were far more than that. They were chamberlains—those charged with the management of the king's means of living. In fact, they were also quartermasters and comptrollers—in the battle against the world, the flesh, and the devil, they were the ones who kept the supply lines open. In the war Jesus conducted against the kingdom of darkness, their material and financial provisioning helped ensure there would be no retreat. Of course, in addition, their presence would have provided emotional sustenance and their prayers contributed to the spiritual rations within the group.

They were faithful unto death. Mary Magdalene and Joanna stand out in the midst of this group of women's names because they were also witnesses of the resurrection.

Furthermore, because Joanna is the Hebrew form of the Latin name, Junia, it is thought she is the apostle mentioned by Paul in his epistle to the Romans:

> *Greet Andronicus and Junia, my fellow countrymen and fellow prisoners. They are outstanding among the apostles, and they were in Christ before I was.*
>
> Romans 16:7 BSB

Some translations describe Andronicus and Junia as 'kinsmen' of Paul—this is because the Greek word can describe either relatives or people of the same nationality. To be an 'apostle' in the early days of the church, there was a requirement to be a witness of the resurrection and to have been with Christ during His ministry on earth. Joanna certainly qualified on both these counts as, of course, did Mary Magdalene.

Sheerah was a city-builder while Bithiah was a nation-builder. They both foreshadowed Mary Magdalene, Susanna and Joanna—the kingdom-builders. Yet there are others in the record of Scripture who heralded the way for women to take up this office of chamberlain and purveyor for the Messiah. The childless woman of Shunem who urged her husband to build a small room on the roof and furnish it with a bed, table, chair and lamp for Elisha so he would have his own quarters whenever he passed through town is one example. The widowed woman of Zarephath who had just enough food for a single meal for herself and her son—and who was asked by Elijah to sacrifice some of it for him—was another. The 'prophet's reward' she called to herself in providing for him was a supernatural supply of oil and flour, sufficient to survive the drought.

Both these women eventually have sons who are taken before their time. And both of them receive their children back from the dead through their faith in God facilitated through the honour they continually gave His prophet. Likewise, Mary and Martha—who provided for Jesus whenever He came through Bethany—received their brother Lazarus back from the dead. Throughout His ministry, it seems that Jesus never stayed overnight in Jerusalem until His arrest. He was always able to retreat to Bethany, just a short distance away, and stay with His friends.

In an earlier age, the female chamberlains, purveyors and providers were women like Abigail who not only supplied David and his men with food but, in doing so, intervened to stop David from committing murder.

In a later age, the female chamberlains, purveyors and providers are women like Lydia of Philippi. She was a trader in fine purple cloth and persuaded Paul and his companions to stay at her house. There, until the time Paul and Silas were imprisoned, they had their needs met through her generosity.

Sometimes God calls the wealthy to be His agents of provision as He did with Lydia and the woman of Shunem. Yet sometimes too it's the utterly destitute—as it was for the widowed woman of Zarephath.

But it is essential to ask God, in these circumstances, if He is the one calling us to this office. Unscrupulous men—and women too—can use Scripture to manipulate our hearts to become chamberlains, supporting their lavish lifestyle rather than their ministry. This may not always be about money—sometimes it's about time, about effort, about attendance, about affirmation. I've been caught out more than once when I thought I was operating in compassion. In reality, my fleshly pity had been hooked on a well-baited line and I was left, flailing desperately, praying for God to rescue me from my lack of due diligence.

God expects us to be stewards of the calling He has given us. That means sometimes making sacrificial gifts of time or money, and sometimes reserving our resources. God never manipulates us; He never tries to shame or pressure us into giving. That is not to say He won't occasionally allow us to feel guilty about our lack of gratitude for His grace—but guilt is a gift that draws us back to Him while shame makes us want to hide from Him. We are never called to sacrifice our own calling for the sake of another's. That is truly terrible stewardship.

We are called to *make* a sacrifice, not *be* a sacrifice. All too often we get confused about the difference. So we have to ask God if we've crossed that boundary and, if we have, repent of stepping into the role of 'saviour'. We're not called to be Jesus to anyone else. And if we try to be, or even if we try to help Jesus out, then we need to realise we don't have faith He is all-sufficient.

Like the father with the boy afflicted by the deaf-mute spirit, we need to cry out, 'Lord, I believe. Help my unbelief.'

Whenever we are pressured to make a sacrifice, almost always the best policy is to wait. Those who wait, said Art Katz, are usually women.[25] Waiting, he adds, is a priestly function.

In many cultures it's unusual to enlist women in frontline warfare. If it's done, there's an effort to eliminate the nurturing, protective instincts of the mother. War is brutal and pitiless and those sensibilities are seen as best left behind. But in the spiritual war Jesus conducted against a cohort of cosmic powers, women were not only valued contributors, they were fellow-travellers with the disciples.

Involving women and allowing them to retain their mothering instincts changes the nature of warfare. It reshapes the dynamic totally.

Some people dismiss the warfare aspect of the ministry of Jesus. Yet that's to ignore His constant conflict with various principalities, dominions and other ungodly powers. When He cast out demons, He was dealing with the footsoldiers of the spirit realm. This was impressive enough to the people of His day, yet He didn't leave it at that lower level.

Many of His miracles are direct assaults on the enemy commanders and dark generals of the powers of the air. His victories were so stunning and unexpected that even His disciples were unsure of the significance of events. Often the battle was over before they even realised it had been declared. On the same day as Jesus claimed the title *Bread of Heaven* from the harvest godling, Tammuz, by multiplying the loaves and fishes, He struck down the pretensions of the consort of Tammuz, the goddess Asherah, who was called *She Who Walks On Water*. When He opened the eyes of the man born blind and thereby claimed the title *The Light of the World*, He was warring against the Persian deity Mithras. When He raised Lazarus from the dead and proclaimed Himself *The Resurrection and the Life*, He was charging into battle with Death and Hell. When He healed the man at the Pool of Bethesda, He was at a pagan shrine—and not for the only time—showing up the impotence of the resident deity. In this case, it was the so-called healer, Asclepius.

These are just a few of the dozens of times Jesus warred against specific unholy rulers in the heavenlies. And while we don't know for sure that women were there on every occasion, we know they were there during His most significant battles: the ones with Hell and Death. They were there at the raising of Lazarus and they were there when He rose from the dead.

They were the purveyors of myrrh and spice to His tomb and, whether they knew it or not, they were—along with Nicodemus—appointed to fulfil the prophecy that spoke of the *'mountains of spices'*. The extraordinary quantity of myrrh brought to the tomb of Jesus was beyond lavish. Mary of Bethany had been severely criticised less than a week earlier for her extravagance in using just one *litra* of anointing oil; but one hundred *litra* were conveyed to the tomb. Not to mention the other spices.

When women are involved in warfare, it changes everything. God knows the heart of woman—He created it, after all. He knows she'd rather protect with a kiss than a kick. That is His own heart's desire too. As we have seen elsewhere in this series, He has devised an extraordinary fusion of the military and the motherly, and gives us His divine armour through a kiss.[26]

The last chapter of the Song of Songs ends with the image of the mountain of spices and the triumph of the young stag—or strong leader—over Death and the grave.

> *Place me like a seal over your heart,*
>   *like a seal on your arm.*
> *For love is as strong as death,*
>   *its jealousy as enduring as the grave.*
> *Love flashes like fire,*
>   *the brightest kind of flame …*
>
>> *Come away, my love! Be like a gazelle*
>> *or a young stag on the mountains of spices.*
>
> Song of Songs 8:6; 14 NLT

We may indeed be called to be chamberlains, providers and purveyors like Joanna or Mary Magdalene, like the widow of Zarephath or the woman of Shunem, like Susannah and Martha or like Abigail and Lydia. However, even if this is not the special office to which God has appointed us, we are still all called to be ministers and purveyors of the Fruit of the Spirit. We are to be provisioners and providers, freely gifting to anyone we meet a fruit salad full of the wondrous flavours of love, joy, peace, patience, kindness, goodness, faithfulness, gentleness and self-control.

In the war against the kingdom of darkness, there are no greater tactical weapons than these. And so long as we keep the supply lines of prayer and praise operational, the Holy Spirit will always be in position. As our Paraclete, He is always with us to ensure the Kingdom of God keeps advancing.

Prayer for myself

Heavenly Father, I'd forgotten my everyday talents: cooking, preparing meals, providing transport, showing others how to do little things. These activities seem so routine, mundane and ordinary that it slipped my mind You'd see them as special. It didn't dawn on me that I might be Your chamberlain for this community.

Sometimes I resent being the one to provide. I find it so hard to remember Your words about love, joy and peace when all around me is chaos and destruction. My first instincts are to return fire with fire. But, Father, I need Your presence and Your wisdom most when the battle rages around me. Hide me from the enemy in Your shadow. I know Your words are truth. I neglect, forget or reject them at my peril, so help me to stay under Your protective covering. Help me to see how significant the simple things of life are to You and how providing them for Your frontline warriors allows the supply lines to remain intact. Remind me that they need me and remind them that they need me.

And we both need You, Father. I ask You to keep my heart clean and give me eyes to see the dangers all around me. Remove the blindness of my heart so I can see clearly the battlelines as they move—the battle between the forces of good and evil. Give me the wisdom to make godly decisions. Give my ears the ability to hear Your clear instructions and the ability to respond appropriately. Give me the words, Lord, to proclaim who You are and Your mighty deeds in this present day and age. Cleanse my heart, Holy Spirit so that it is a fit place for You to be my Paraclete and my Protector.

In the name of Jesus of Nazareth. Amen.

Prayer for others

Father, I lift to You my friends and my family, my colleagues and loved ones, my neighbours and my community. I ask You to watch over their dreams and shepherd them on the pathway towards their fulfillment. I ask You to provision their visions. I ask You to bind up their crushed faith and their broken hearts and heal those wounds that have stolen their hopes from them.

I particularly ask You, Lord, to guide those You have appointed as chamberlains and purveyors to walk in the calling You have placed on their hearts. Lord, connect them with those of Your people You want them to maintain supply lines for. Grant them wisdom, initiative, skills of navigation and discernment—so that, whatever the spiritual battle, they are the back-up force that enables the ground that has been won to be held. Whether it's prayer or listening support, whether it's money or skills, give them the power to declare: 'No retreat!'

Lord, You have gifted all of us with many and valuable gifts. Many of us are talented beyond compare and over-ready to step into our calling. However, we neither recognise these blessings nor utilise them. Open our eyes, Lord, to be able to see what You have done for us—that we are blessed to be a blessing, that we are favoured to spread favour, that we are provisioners of the vision.

Teach us, Father, that we are the Chamberlains, the Paradigm-shifters, the Nation-shapers and the City-builders of this age. Teach us, Lord, that time is meaningless to You. Yesterday has passed. Tomorrow has not come. There is only now. And we ask You to transform the time of the present in the eternal now of Your presence. Become to us Immanuel, God with us.

In the name of Jesus of Nazareth. Amen.

5
Woman and Mother: Torch-Bearer

5
Woman and Mother: Torch-Bearer

> *EVERY HUMAN BEING NEEDS TO understand on the deepest level that within them is a lit candle. And no two people's candles are alike. And there is no person who doesn't have a candle. Every human being needs to know and understand that they must work to discover how to share their candlelight with others, and to ignite it into a mighty torch that illuminates the entire world.*
>
> Abraham Isaac Kook[27]

In the era before the kings came to power in Israel, women still had names.[28] And there, in the hill country of Ephraim, lived a prophet whose name has echoed down through history: Deborah.

It was a time of great social chaos. Joshua, the great commander who was the successor to Moses, had died. So too had his stalwart supporter, Caleb—but not before taking the city of those giants who had so intimidated ten of the twelve spies nearly half a century previously.

For forty years Caleb's nephew Othniel had continued the legacy of his uncle and also of Joshua, defending the people against incursions by land-hungry rulers and their warlords. Then he too died.

He was the first of the judges and, although he was obviously a great warrior, there is no evidence he was a military strategist in the mould of Joshua. Nor, it seems, were those who came immediately after him. It was Deborah who revived the role of the war tactician.

In her day, community life had completely broken down. Danger stalked the roads. People who had to travel for any reason went by circuitous back routes. The highways were abandoned. Even when war was right on their doorstep, the villagers of Israel refused to fight. They'd rather appease their enemies than try to protect themselves. So, for more than twenty years, they were brutally oppressed by Jabin, the king of Hazor in Upper Galilee. They were so downtrodden that even the idea of defence was unimaginable. As for an attack on their enemies, that was utterly unthinkable.

But then the Lord gave Deborah a war plan.

> *Deborah, a prophet, the wife of Lappidoth, was leading Israel at that time. She held court under the Palm of Deborah between Ramah and Bethel in the hill country of Ephraim, and the Israelites went up to her to have their disputes decided. She sent for Barak son of Abinoam from Kedesh in Naphtali and said to him, 'The Lord, the God of Israel, commands you: "Go, take with you ten thousand men of Naphtali and Zebulun and lead them up to Mount Tabor. I will lead Sisera, the commander*

> *of Jabin's army, with his chariots and his troops to the Kishon River and give him into your hands.'"*

Judges 4:4–7 NIV

Barak was, to say the very least, not keen on this idea. Perhaps he thought it was all very well for Deborah to announce the Word of the Lord to him when it didn't involve any risk on her part—but it might be a different matter if her life was on the line. So he asked her to come with him.

Now the Hebrew text tells us that Deborah was a Lapidot-woman, *a torch-wife*. That may simply mean that, as every English version translates it, she was married to a man named Lappidoth. Jewish commentaries are less sure about her marital status, viewing it as quite strange that Lappidoth doesn't appear in the story at all. Instead they see a possible alternative rendering for the unusual phrase 'Lapidot-woman'. This is *torchbearer*—a woman of fire, a lamplighter, a fire-kindler.[29]

Torch-bearer is suggestive of a wordplay that fits a pattern for biblical names: Deborah is the *torch* who ignites Barak, *the lightning*. Together they prepared for battle. Barak was reluctant and refused to muster an army unless she came with him into combat. So Deborah accompanied him back to his home town.

As a pair they are not just God's appointed envoys for the task of rescuing His people, but a living contrast to the heralds of the storm-god worshipped in neighbouring lands. The *Epic of Gilgamesh* contains the flood story of Mesopotamia and appearing in it are two minor godlings, Sullat[30] the *torch* and Hanish the *lightning*. In the *Epic*, they are harbingers of destruction by water. They are accompanied by seven lords of the heavens[31] who bring torches to set fire to the land.

Similarly Deborah and Barak are God's agents of destruction by water: a rushing torrent from the river Kishon overtakes Sisera's iron chariots and leads to his defeat. In addition, the Israelite forces receive heavenly assistance as testified by Deborah in her song:

> *From the heavens the stars fought; from their courses they fought against Sisera.*
>
> Judges 5:20 BSB

The Hebrew word for *their courses*, 'mesullatam', looks seriously like a play on the name Sullat, that attendant of the storm god. It's as if Deborah is saying: did our enemies really think their godlings were a match for Yahweh of Israel? No, indeed! They bow before Him. They do His bidding.

The *torch* and the *lightning* are servants of Yahweh, not of the nations. The *torch* is in fact His covenant symbol.

> *When the sun had gone down and it was dark, behold, a smoking fire pot and a flaming torch passed between these pieces. On that day the Lord made a covenant with Abram, saying, 'To your offspring I give this land, from the river of Egypt to the great river, the river Euphrates, the land of the Kenites, the Kenizzites, the Kadmonites, the Hittites, the Perizzites, the Rephaim, the Amorites, the Canaanites, the Girgashites and the Jebusites.'*
>
> Genesis 15:17–21 ESV

In Deborah's time, this promise of God looked to be broken. The Canaanites were ascendant and had been for decades. God had promised the land to the children of Abraham as their inheritance. Instead the king of Hazor was crushing them down.

It was Deborah who re-ignited hope in this covenant word of the Lord, fanning the last almost-dead embers of faith amongst the subjugated Israelites. But, as she noted, not everyone responded.

> *'Awake, awake, Deborah: awake, awake, utter a song.'*
>
> Judges 5:12 KJV

<u>Utter</u> a song: *speak* a song: *prophesy* a song. The word in Hebrew is 'dabar' and is the root of the name Deborah. It was the people of God going down to the gates who called Deborah to fulfil the prophecy within her own name.

> *Awake, awake, Deborah; awake, awake, utter a song; rise, Barak, and take your captivity captive, Son of Abinoam.*
>
> Judges 5:12 LSV

This should remind us of Jesus who fulfilled the prophecy within the psalms, quoted by Paul:

> *To each one of us grace was given according to the measure of Christ's gift. Therefore He says:*
> *'When He ascended on high,*
> *He led captivity captive,*
> *And gave gifts to men.'*
>
> Ephesians 4:7–8 NKJV,
> quoting Psalm 68:18

Christ is able not just to free us from our physical bonds but from the very mental strongholds that keep us bound: He can take captive the mindset the keeps us in captivity.

That's the very outlook, the frame of thinking, that Deborah had to torch. She had to set fire to a lie that the people of her time believed—life will be easier if we stay captive than if we fight for liberty. It's easy for us to have a similar attitude and demur in supporting the defenders of our freedom. In her song, Deborah named those tribes who were happy to benefit from the actions of those who resisted tyranny but were not willing to risk themselves. And in his essay, *Live Not By Lies*, Aleksander Solzhenitsyn said, 'He who is not sufficiently courageous to defend his soul… let him say to himself, "I am a part of the herd and a coward. It's all the same to me as long as I'm fed and kept warm."'

It's that kind of complacency Deborah had to burn to the ground. Calling for Barak, summoning him to her side and then accompanying him home to begin the troop muster, she constantly wielded a mighty weapon. This was the word of God. She might have been a *torch-wife* but her name, Deborah, means *speak, declare, proclaim, promise*.

But before she could fulfill her destiny as God's prophet and His battle tactician, she herself had to be stirred from slumber. 'Awake, awake!' the people said to her.

It should remind us of a story Jesus told about torch-bearers and the importance of remaining awake.

> *At that time the kingdom of heaven will be like ten virgins who took their lamps and went out to meet the bridegroom. Five of them were foolish and five were*

wise. The foolish ones took their lamps but did not take any oil with them. The wise ones, however, took oil in jars along with their lamps. The bridegroom was a long time in coming, and they all became drowsy and fell asleep.

At midnight the cry rang out: 'Here's the bridegroom! Come out to meet him!'

Then all the virgins woke up and trimmed their lamps. The foolish ones said to the wise, 'Give us some of your oil; our lamps are going out.'

'No,' they replied, 'there may not be enough for both us and you. Instead, go to those who sell oil and buy some for yourselves.'

But while they were on their way to buy the oil, the bridegroom arrived. The virgins who were ready went in with him to the wedding banquet. And the door was shut.

Later the others also came. 'Lord, Lord,' they said, 'open the door for us!'

But he replied, 'Truly I tell you, I don't know you.'

Therefore keep watch, because you do not know the day or the hour.

Matthew 25:1–13 NIV

There are ten 'torch-bearers', 'lamp-lighters', 'fire-kindlers' in this parable. Ten women charged with the task of lighting the way for the Bridegroom. Only five of them fulfill their appointed role. They couldn't keep watch, they couldn't wait. Remember what Art Katz said? That those who wait are usually women. And that waiting is a priestly function.

Perhaps, we might think, we've been so careless and inattentive at waiting, the door has shut on us. Perhaps, we think, it's too late. There are two things to remember if we're tempted to believe that. First, that Jesus of Nazareth, who is both Lord and God, is the redeemer of wasted time. And secondly:

> *The gifts and the calling of God are irrevocable.*
>
> Romans 11:29 NKJV

Whatever spiritual office God appoints us to, He will never withdraw it. We may be called to be a city-builder like Sheerah, a nation-shaper like Bithiah, a purveyor like Joanna, a paradigm-shifter like the daughters of Zelophehad, a tactician like Deborah. The destiny God has prepared for us is unalterable and unchangeable. This doesn't mean to say we are fated to achieve it, just that He will never change His mind about it, no matter how late in life we leave it.

Whatever spiritual gifts have been bestowed upon us so that we can discharge this calling and destiny, God won't ever demand them back. They wouldn't be *gifts* otherwise. What we do with His gifts is up to us. We can use them, abuse them or waste them.

This is why we can sometimes be deceived when we see others operating at a high level of gifting. We think they must be godly—because we assume that, if they were behaving in an immoral way, God would remove the gift. Not so. The gift, like the calling, is irrevocable.

Jesus tells us how to discern a follower of His, and it's not by the gifts, but by the fruit:

> *Just as you can identify a tree by its fruit, so you can identify people by their actions.*
>
> Matthew 7:20 NLT

So, use your gift.

Discover your calling. Step into the vocation that God has been asking you to accept.

Make a difference.

Change the world.

Summon the future.

Light the way.

Awake, awake.

Awake, awake, daughter of destiny!

Prayer for myself

Father of all, I know I have Deborah-like abilities, talents and passion. I have the torch inside. Help my lack of ability to kindle others with that light. I don't know if I'm lazy, inept or just reliant on my own power rather than a conductor of the fire of Your Spirit. But I know You inspire and motivate the lazy, the inept and the self-reliant. Father, so often I let my feelings of inadequacy reign and I tend to ignore any stirrings in my spirit.

Are those stirrings from You, Father, calling my spirit into life—life with You? Is that You calling me forth from my slumber and into my destiny—the role You had in mind for me before the beginning of the earth? Father, please fan the dying embers of my lack of passion into the blazing fire I need so as to become Your torch-bearer in my corner of the world. I am so frightened of authority and resistant to it. I am frightened by and resistant to being that authority. I am so unworthy.

And I am sure I heard You say: *You are right. You are unworthy. But your faith in Jesus, My Son, makes you worthy. Do you think Deborah found it easy to get started? No, she didn't any more than you will. But with Jesus at your side and the Holy Spirit to inspire and motivate you, nothing I ask of you—absolutely nothing—is beyond you and Me together. Go forth in peace and put your hand in the hand of Jesus and together fight the good fight for the sake of My kingdom.*

And so, Lord, I pray that Jesus will take my hand and wrap His prayer shawl around me so that I am covered with His prayers of love and protection. I pray that the Holy Spirit will guide my heart and mind as I bear Your torch of love to honour and glorify You.

In Jesus' name. Amen.

Prayer for others

Heavenly Father, I honour You and I ask You to glorify Your name through me. May Your name be kept as holy as it is in heaven.

I come before You and plead for my sisters—my relatives, friends, neighbours, colleagues and fellow travelling companions. They are very little different from me and together we make a sad bunch of 'gunnas'. We want to and are always 'gunna'—going to—do mighty deeds for Your kingdom. We're like Barak, not Deborah. We need a fire-starter to kindle us into flame. Our intentions are good—but we all know which road is paved by good intentions.

Father, please re-ignite the pilot light of our understanding so that women everywhere can understand what it means to come under authority while at the same time becoming a leader with authority others will want to follow. Lord, we are leaders—help our lack of leadership.

Father, teach every woman who thinks it is too late that it is never too late—just because it hasn't happened, for whatever reason, does not mean it will not happen. You are the redeemer of wasted time. You are never in a hurry and You are the God of the impossible and the God of the second, third and fourth chances.

Just because we are lazy, unmotivated, inadequate, scared, and just because our get-up-and-go has got-up-and-gone, it does not have to remain that way. Empower us all,

Father, to become the best we can be for the sake of Your kingdom. Make us to be like Deborah—Deborah who fought to set the captives free—free from the captivity of their minds. Deborah was in many ways was a forerunner of Your Son, Jesus of Nazareth.

We ask these blessings and this favour in the name of Jesus, our Redeemer. Amen.

Endnotes

1. It may also have a subtle overtone of 'shor', *cattle*, the cause of the misfortune. In addition, Sheerah may mean *near kinswoman* or *flesh*, or *blood relative*. It's most widely regarded as being from 'shaar', *remnant* or *left over*, which has nuances of 'seor', *leaven*, of which a small remnant was always kept for the next batch of bread. It may also have been meant to evoke singing. *I will sing* is 'ashirah' and, although the spelling is different—'ashirah' having a yod, while Sheerah has the letter aleph—puns are so frequent in Hebrew, it's wise not to ignore the possibility. And of course, if we move the letter aleph in Sheerah's name to the front, the name of the goddess Asherah emerges.

2. Dr Wil Gafney calls Sheerah a 'smith' at wilgafney.com/2020/07/15/building-on-sheerahs-legacy/ (accessed 5 April 2021)

3. Rev. Willem Glashouwer says in his devotional commentary on Revelation that it is remarkable the first city-builders were descendants of Cain. 'City builders are also named among the descendants of the cursed Ham. Israel was a nation of shepherds and farmers. Jerusalem is also a large city, of course, but the prophet says that Jerusalem will be inhabited as a town without walls. Massing people together leads to a lot of injustice. The present world cities are a living proof of this, with their murders, theft, debauchery and smog—human anthills, urban jungles, where the law of the fittest rules.'

4. Cain seems to have built it in Nod, while Sheerah has built her cities in Canaan during a time when the vast majority of her relatives are living in Egypt.

5. Covenants after all were ratified by the use of the body of an animal, divided into two with an area to walk in between the parts.

6. Everything, apparently, could be sacrificed to Horon except a goat. See Karel van der Toorn, Bob Becking, Pieter W. Van der Horst, *Dictionary of Deities and Demons in the Bible*, Brill 1999

7   https://www.washingtonpost.com/world/meet-rashida-tlaibs-grandma-who-wouldnt-be-proud-of-a-granddaughter-like-that/2019/08/16/f90b055e-bf97-11e9-a8b0-7ed8a0d5dc5d_story.html (accessed 29 January 2021)

8   https://www.abarim-publications.com/Meaning/Beth-horon.html (accessed 30 January 2021)

9   Talmud Sanhedrin 32b.

10 jewishweek.timesofisrael.com/counting-sheep-on-rosh-hashanah/ comments: 'On Rosh Hashanah, all the inhabitants of the world pass before God like B'nei Maron, as it is written, "He Who creates all their hearts as one, Who understands all their deeds." (Psalms 33:15)' B'nei Maron has long been thought to be a reference to Beth Horon, as pointed out at oztorah.com/2019/10/the-bnei-maron/ (accessed 2 February 2021)

11 The dramatic High Holyday poem, Une'tanneh Tokef, written in the Middle Ages and possibly emanating from Rabbi Amnon of Mainz.

12 She was apparently the sister of Beriah who was the father of Rephah, the father of Resheph, the father of Telah, the father of Tahan, the father of Ladan, the father of Ammihud, the father of Elishama, the father of Nun, the father of Joshua. However, the text is somewhat ambiguous, so she might be Beriah's daughter and the sister of Rephah. That would remove one 'great-' from the ancestral description in relation to Joshua.

13 Or more accurately, the rotation of the earth slowed to a standstill. The only thing capable of doing this in the natural would have been a massive celestial body moving in very close to earth orbit: a giant comet, perhaps, which would explain the stones falling from heaven. Although many translations suggest these stones were hailstones, I personally believe they were meteorites. The Hebrew word for them, 'barad', seems basically to mean *lightning stones*—which could refer to storms and thus *hailstones* or alternatively could mean *firestones* which would point to meteorites. Take your pick.

Some commentators suggest that the sun did not stand still—but that the event was an annular eclipse. (See, for example, jpost.com/Israel-News/Miracle-described-in-Book-of-Joshua-may-have-been-earliest-recorded-solar-eclipse-510903 —accessed 22 June 2021). Now, while the word for 'stand still' could be also be interpreted 'go dumb' or 'stop shining', it seems unlikely Joshua would have wanted to fight in the dark. Furthermore it is difficult to explain the sun positioned over Gibeon and thus east of Beth Horon, while the moon is south-west of Beth Horon over the valley of Aijalon. This particular positioning indicates that the moon would have been a waning crescent, past its three-quarter phase. It would therefore have risen on the eastern horizon in the very early hours of the morning—between midnight and dawn—and be headed towards its setting in the west in the afternoon.

One further reason I am inclined to doubt this was an eclipse, either annular or total, is because Isaiah refers to this event as an 'alien work' of God—something so strange and abnormal as to be virtually unthinkable. An eclipse was far from unthinkable—in fact, by the time of Isaiah or thereabouts, they were eminently predictable. The magi of Babylon—whose work included both astronomy and astrology—were able to calculate their appearance with great accuracy. Their name for the eclipse cycle was 'saros' and it is a term still used today.

14   *Constitutions* of Thomas Arundel, Archbishop of Canterbury, 1409

15   These names include 'Yequthiel', *obedience to God* or *God will nourish* or *God is hope*. The other traditional names assigned to Moses in the writings of the sages are: Yered, *descent*; Avigdor, *master of the fence*; Chever, *companion*; Avi Socho, *father of seers*; Avi Zanoach, *master of rejection*; Toviah, *goodness*; Shemayeh ben Nethanel, t*he listener to whom God gave* (the Torah); Ben Evyatar, *son of pardon*; Levi, from his tribe. See chabad.org/parshah/article_cdo/aid/627663/jewish/What-Was-Moshes-Real-Name.htm (accessed 8 June 2021)

16   Moses has an obvious kinship with Egyptian names like Thutmose, Ramose, Ptahmose, Ahmose and Amenmose. These names integrate that of a deity and proclaim: child of Thoth, born of Ra, shaped by Ptah, son of Iah and offspring of Amon. Based on this similarity and because 'mo' means *water*, Moses may also have the sense *child of the river-god* or *son of the Nile*.

17   *The Nelson Study Bible*, Thomas Nelson Inc 1997

18   This is not to say that God didn't try to give Moses a Hebrew name and to raise a name covenant with him that included a non-Egyptian name. I believe Moses consistently refused this covenant offered by God. For more details on this name covenant and its

implication for Moses not being able to enter the Promised Land, see *Dealing with Azazel: Spirit of Rejection*, Armour Books 2021

19 She married Mered (1 Chronicles 4:18) and became the mother of Miriam, Shammai and Ishbah. Mered means *rebel*. Some of the Jewish sages consider Mered to be a nickname for Caleb, the stalwart companion of Joshua who, forty-five years after he'd visited Hebron and seen its dangers, still believed in God's promise that it could be taken. Caleb was classed as a *rebel* because he did not agree with his ten fellow spies who said that the giants in the Promised Land made it impossible to conquer.

20 Also spelled Bitya, from BatYa ('Bat', *daughter*, and 'Ya' from 'Yah' or 'Yahweh', *God*)

21 There may also be five at the cross but it's very difficult to be sure. Present at the crucifixion were 'many women' which from the varying descriptions lies somewhere between four and seven: Mary the mother of Jesus, Mary Magdalene, Mary the mother of James and Joseph, Salome who may be the same as the mother of the sons of Zebedee, the sister or sister-in-law of Jesus' mother who may be the same as Mary of Clopas.

22 Michal may also have been barren. It's unclear whether she was infertile or whether David simply refused to have anything to do with her after she confronted him about his shameless dancing. Certainly she did not give birth, as these others did. Elizabeth is another woman who was barren but she too eventually gave birth; however she is not included in this count because her story is not part of the Hebrew portion of the Scriptures.

23 Sheerah's first cousin was Makir, son of Manasseh. Makir's son was Gilead and his son was Hepher and his was Zelophedad.

24 These name meanings are all from the Biblical names database at Abarim Publications. See abarim-publications.com.

25 Art Katz, *The Anatomy of Deception*, Burning Bush Press, 2008

26 The concept of putting on the armour of God by receiving His kiss of protection is a concept embedded in the Hebrew understanding of armour and is implied in Paul's description in Ephesians 6. For more detail, see *More Precious than Pearls: The Mother's Blessing and God's Favour Towards Women*, Armour Books 2016 See also *God's Panoply: The Armour of God and the Kiss of Heaven*, Armour Books 2016

27 Abraham Isaac Kook was the First Ashkenazic chief rabbi of pre-state Israel (1865–1935).

28 See *As Resplendent As Rubies: The Mother's Blessing and God's Favour Towards Women II*, Armour Books 2020 for more on the loss and regaining of women's names in Scripture. The book of Genesis documents the names of 25 women, five lots of five. These are, in order: Eve, Adah, Zillah, Naamah, Sarai/Sarah, Milcah, Hagar, Rebekah, Reumah, Keturah, Judith, Basemath, Mahalath, Rachel, Leah, Zilpah, Bilhah, Dinah, Deborah, Adah, Oholibamah, Timna, Mehetabel, Tamar and Asenath. It's possible there may be two women named Timna. There are also other unnamed women: Potiphar's wife and Lot's daughters, for example. However, far more women are named than remain unnamed. As time progresses towards the era of the kings, the reverse is true: many more women are unnamed than are named. A renewed recognition of women through the recording of their names only begins once again during the time of Jesus.

29 See, for example, https://www.myjewishlearning.com/article/deborah/

30 Also spelled 'Tsullat'. He was an attendant of the sun god as well as a bodyguard of the storm god

31 These are known as the Anunnaki. Over time, they are also referred to as gods of the underworld or, more specifically, as seven judges of the underworld.

In this series

Each book in this series can be read independently.

The first volume, *More Precious than Pearls*, highlights the admiration of many Jewish writers for the women of the Exodus. They were remarkable women of steadfast, tested faith: armour-bearers, watchmen, game-changers, gatekeepers and cupbearers.

The second volume, *As Resplendent as Rubies*, explores the role of Biblical women who were kingmakers, visionaries, navigators, sentinels, mentors, culture-changers and even God-namers.

This third volume, *As Exceptional as Sapphires*, is about the women builders—the purveyors and chamberlains, nation-shapers, torch-bearers and paradigm-shifters.

The gifts and offices of God are irrevocable, so it is wise to learn the Scriptural principles behind these divine appointments as we seek to live out the call of God on our lives.

Jesus and the Healing of History

The patterns of the past are locked into the landscape. People need healing, but so does the land. Every location mentioned in the ministry of Jesus is profoundly significant. Where a placename is revealed in relation to the healing of a person, then—if it is possible to examine the background of that place—we realise that people, land and history are simultaneously being healed.

When Jesus went to Sychar and met the woman at the well, He went to the specific location where the kingdom passed down from David was ripped in two. And in being proclaimed 'the Messiah', He reunited the divided kingdom. Five momentous covenants were enacted at this place, so it is no wonder a five-times-married woman represents its history.

Jesus and the Healing of History is a series that delves into the background of the localities where Jesus performed His miracles. Each book is lavishly illustrated in full-colour.

www.ingramcontent.com/pod-product-compliance
Lightning Source LLC
Chambersburg PA
CBHW071529080526
44588CB00011B/1610